Annita's
Stories
of
Africa

Love
Annita

Annita's Stories of Africa

By Annita Cole

ANNITA'S STORIES OF AFRICA

Published by Annita Cole, Edmonton, Canada

ISBN:

Paperback	978-1-77354-580-6
ebook	978-1-77354-587-5

Publication assistance and digital printing in Canada by

PUBLISHING
PageMaster.ca

Thank You to Anna-Lisa, a dear friend of our family, for editing these stories. Your editing business "Arbordel Editing" has made these stories of my experiences possible.

Contents

Introduction

My name is Annita Helen Cole and I was born on a small farm southeast of Rocky Mountain House close to Chedderville, Alberta, Canada.

When I was twelve years old, God spoke to me audibly and told me to get ready to teach children in Africa.

I took my training at Prairie Bible Institute in Three Hills , Alberta which isn't far from Rocky Mt. House. After this I took a winter at the Full Gospel Bible School in Eston Saskatchewan. It took another year and then God showed me I was to go to Malawi Africa to teach there. I went out there under the Apostolic Church of Pentecost. My co-worker was Isabel Duncan.

The stories in this series are based on the things that happened there.

The Malawians were wonderful and very generous with time and anything they had. It was a different world from what I grew up in and yet a lot the same.

I would like the children to see that God calls children like them and gives them gifts to serve Him with. God also enables His children to do what he has called them to do. Our God is faithful. 1 Corinthians 1:9 " God is faithful by whom ye were called unto the fellowship of His Son,Jesus Christ , our Lord.

Also "faithful is He who calleth you who also will do it" 1 Thessalonians 5:24

Annita Cole

The Fire

Northern Malawi- language -Tumbuka

Hi kids, I'm Patty Peugeot! I'm owned by humans called Izzy and Neatie. Right now my tires are carrying us over a sandy road to Northern Malawi. It's a long, dusty , tiring trip which takes most of the day. I make the trip with them every year. We come up here to give bible studies to the adults and children.

We are nearing Ncena Cena in the late afternoon. We are all very tired. The humans here were very happy to see us. They have been busy while waiting for us today. They made a new outside kitchen and toilet made of elephant grass .Izzy said they would sleep in me and cook under the sky in the kitchen. As I stopped and the dust settled I heard a gurgle and saw a lovely little stream flowing by the village not far from us.There were banana trees by the stream.I think we will all sleep well tonight.

Neatie put an apple box up on end to put the one burner stove on. As she was getting the coal oil stove going , the fire that was warming the stove up dropped in the elephant grass. I was really scared because if that fire got away it would burn me up. It would also burn the stacked grass to put on the mud houses , and then burn the grass roofs off the houses in the

Annita Cole

village. The hen sitting on chicks in the apple box was very brave. She didn't move at all while the fire was burning around her. She was willing to give her life for her babies. Neatie finally got the fire out to the relief of all of us.

We stayed here for two weeks and had a great time. I carried everyone to the different villages every afternoon. Neatie, Izzy and a few others gave out the gospel of Jesus.

When Neatie needed to go to the toilet, there was a small grass enclosure with a hole to do her business in.When she came close to the grass hut, called a chimbuzi,she cleared her throat. If she hears someone clear their throat inside she knows someone is in there. If no one clears their throat she knows it is empty and she can go in.

The people here speak Tumbuka so she doesn't know what they are saying.When she teaches, someone who knows both English and Tumbuka will tell the people what she is saying.

Neatie is giving the kids a story every day and also teaches the adults.

Everyone needs the privilege to hear that Jesus is God and came to the earth in the flesh, ministered to the people and then died and rose again to free the humans from their sin. John 3:16 . Neatie told the kids about the hen who was willing to give her life for her babies. It reminded me of how Jesus came to earth to give up his life for all the humans. They have a job to do also. They need to repent of their sin and ask Jesus to forgive them. When they do this they are forgiven and become part of God's family,

The very long day is over and Neatie and Izzy made their bed , locked my doors. and went to sleep. Bye for now ,I'm falling asleep and I'll talk to you again.

a New Experience

Hi kids, I'm back again. I see a lot of things from my parking place by the nice little stream that is going by. Neatie needed a bath and a lady came with a dish of water and put it in a grass bath house. This bath place didn't have a roof. When Neatie went in she carried her soap and a towel. I could see she was uncomfortable as she could see heads going by and they could see her head. As people went by they were greeting her and she was saying hi back.If you kids get a chance to have a bath in an outside bath house made of elephant grass you should do it. The sun is beating down on your head, the wind is blowing and you get to chat with friends.

The women had hauled water and warmed it for everyone. Neatie told Izzy she admired them very much for their hard work and hospitality. By the time we left Neatie had gotten used to bathing in a public area and enjoyed it.

One day Neatie was walking along the gurgling stream and saw a freshwater crab. She said that was the first time she had seen one. There are lots of banana trees here as well . The last day came and they packed me up again . It is a very beautiful area. It reminds me of Gen 1: 31 where God looked over all he had made, and he saw that it was very good! If you look at the first few chapters of Genesis you will see that God made everything.

I hope I can come here again next year. Good-bye for now and you can be sure I'll talk to you again.

the Heart that Stopped

Hi kids, I'm back to tell you another story. When we were finished at Nchena Chena, the humans packed up their things , loaded me up , climbed in and we left for home. After traveling for hours it was starting to get dark and I knew something was wrong.I couldn't keep going and my heart stopped. The humans

Annita Cole

were startled and became very concerned. They needed to get home and we were miles from where we lived. The humans prayed and then sat talking about what to do. One of the ministers said he thought there was a bush hospital a mile down the road. It was then decided that one would walk to the car hospital and the other stay with Izzy and Neatie.

We sat for a very long time but finally saw the flash light coming. When Amhango arrived he said he found it and they would come when they were done with the job they were doing. An hour later they came and fixed me and I felt my heart beating again. The energy flowed through me and it was a comfort to feel normal again. We started out again and after traveling a very long time we finally arrived home . I was sure glad I didn't have any more heart trouble.

As I sat parked at the mission house door I was thinking about the day. I realized that God had answered prayer that day. James 1:6 tells us that we should pray without doubting . We prayed and God heard us and rescued us out of our troubles,

I'm tired so I am going to go to sleep. Don't worry, I'll tell you another story soon. Good night.

the Help God Sent

Hi kids, I'm a dark blue Peugoet called Peggy and I belong to Izzy. Neatie just joined us a few weeks ago and we live in Malawi at Mpanda Mission. Today we are going to Chimbudzi. It's a village about ten miles from our home.

The road is sandy but I'm doing fine and Izzy is a good driver.We arrive and visit the chief. After a bit we go to visit a friend at a canteen (coffee shop). Izzy and Neatie go in and visit for a while. I just rested and watched the people come and go.When they came out Neatie put the key in my heart and turned it but it wouldn't start beating. Neatie opened my chest but couldn't see anything wrong. I heard them praying for help. Soon I saw dust coming toward us and Neatie jumped out of me and flagged the car down. I recognized my mechanic friend from the hospital they take me to in Lilongwe. I don't know who was happier, Neatie or Me. The mechanic worked on me for ten minutes and my heart started up again. Neatie and Izzy thanked God for answering our prayer.

On our way home I thought about how Jesus is always with us. He always knows what's happening to us . Hebrews 13:5 tells us that He never leaves us or forsakes us. It was Jesus

Annita Cole

who put that Mechanic in the same place as us when we needed help. We didn't have any more trouble that day and got home safely.

a Lion Nearby

Hi kids! Remember Patty Peugeot? Hope you do because I have another story for you.

Izzy, Neatie, and two pastors got into me and we started down the road to Ntcheu. My tires were new, I was filled up with energy, and I was all cleaned up.

Annita Cole

There were people, dogs, cows, chickens, sheep and other cars on the road. I have to really pay attention that I don't bump into any of them.

We turned off the main road onto a dirt road to reach Ntceu. I was pulling a tent trailer so when we arrived at the church , Izzy and Neatie unhooked me and set up the tent.

The people were happy to see us when they arrived from their village close by. They were singing as they came. We had our first teaching classes and then every one had Nsima ndi Ndiwo. This means they had corn porridge and a vegetable.

After supper a man came to tell us that there was a lion ten miles from us. That seems like a long way away but lions can travel a long way in one night. The people went home to the village to sleep in their houses. They wanted us to come with them but we didn't think a lion would come close because of the smell of my energy. (gasoline)

We were fine the next morning and the people came back for more classes.

Neatie and Izzy believe God answers prayer. 1 Thessalonians 5 :17 says we are to pray without ceasing. They trusted him to look after them and He did. It's hot here and I noticed Neatie ate a lot of Papaya. We stayed three days and then returned to our home at Mponela.

I'll be talking to you again

the Visitor in the Night

Well here I am again kids and I want to tell you about a visitor in the night.

Izy parked me by the tent trailer not far from Lake Malawi where we were to have bible studies for a weekend. Izzy and Neatie had gone to bed and as far as I know were sound asleep; when I saw this very skinny dog going into the tent. I worried about this as sometimes skinny animals are that way because they have rabies.

This disease makes them very angry and they will bite anything they can. I listened but didn't hear anything so I went to sleep.

I was awakened by a noisy fight in the morning.Neatie had a broom and was trying to chase the dog out of the tent. It didn't want to go as it had found a cozy place to sleep. It was putting up a fight but Neatie didn't give up and soon the dog came running out of the tent and down the road. It didn't bite her and so all was well.

She was definitely fine as I saw her playing soccer with the kids before classes.

This made me think of how we have Jesus with us at all times. If we have asked Jesus to forgive our sin and wash us clean then we are God's children . The Holy Spirit is with us at all times to help and protect us. Ps 91:14 The Lord says"I will rescue those who love me. I will protect those who trust in my Name."

the Miracle

Hi kids! Patty Peauguot is back. I have another story for you of how good God is. It is a very sunny day with a slight breeze blowing. We are headed for an area we don't visit often so I am excited to see what the country and people are like.

We are traveling over a lot of hills and valleys. We are coming to some windy roads that are very narrow. The sides of the road are higher than the road and so you can't see very far to the left and the right. The dust is flying up behind my tires and all of a sudden I see a bicycle from up the top of a hill on the right side a little ahead of us. It was really going and Izzy stomped on my brakes real hard. I screeched and screamed real loud. We were slowing down quickly and a good thing as we hit the man behind his foot on the back wheel. Oh my he is flying into the ditch bicycle and all.

Izzy and Neatie get out and rush to him and he is saying he is sorry over and over again. Then people from his village over the hill he came down arrived. They see he is fine and give him trouble for not fixing his brakes. At this point he says Pepani , Pepani, Pepani ndithu. This means sorry, sorry, sorry indeed.

My left light shield was broken but the man is fine and not even one spoke from the wheel of the bike is bent or broken. I hear everyone say

Annita Cole

that it is a miracle from God that this man's life was saved. I think about this the rest of the way home . Psalm 91:2 says that God is our refuge and fortress. In him we will trust. He certainly protected us today in what could have been a terrible accident. The man is still alive and we are on our way home with only a broken left light. How good God is.

Thump, Thump

Thump! Thump! Thud! Thud! What is going on in the house ? Wish someone would tell me. I'm Peggy Peaugot and they left me sitting outside the back door. Sometimes they park me in the garage but most of the time I'm outside. Right now I'm hearing this thudding and thumping and I can't figure out what is going on.

Neatie comes outside and hollers for a young man standing near me. She says Njoka! (snake) come quick and bring a stick. He gets a stick and runs in the house. The suspense is killing me. Did they get it or didn't they? After a bit they come out of the house with a dead green mwamba on a stick. They tell people nearby that it came through the dining room window , onto the table and then the floor. Neatie heard the noise and ran to see what it was. Instead of waiting to see where it went she ran to get help and when they got back they didn't see it. After looking for a bit they found it behind a cupboard in the hall. When they thumped the cupboard it's head came up and they killed it.

We are all thankful that Neatie heard the snake and that they were able to find it. You only have fifteen minutes to get the antidote if a green or black mwamba bites you..

I heard Neatie say that the Lord keeps watch over you as you come and go. It is found in Psalms 121:8

Annita Cole

Snakes that Spit

My engine roared and my tires flew over the ground. Neatie needed to get home in a hurry. I pulled up by the house and Neatie ran to the little room at the end of the porch. I saw the door close and then open again. Neatie shouted Njoka (snake) and ran for a stick by the house. The door opened and shut again and in time she came out and told us a spitting cobra had spit at her when she rushed in the first time. It had spit at her watch instead of her eyes so she was fine. The second time she went in the cobra was gone. There was a hole in the wall so Neatie filled it up with cement.

She then told us of another time when she got out a binder from under her bed to get at some lessons she wanted to teach. There was a small spitting cobra in the space where the rings are in the binder. She carried the box outside but the cobra got away from her.That time also the snake spit at her watch instead of her eyes.

Spitting cobras spit at the eyes of their enemies so they can get away while the enemy can't see them. The antidote for the spit is milk. I watched Neaties dog,Chief, after a spitting cobra spit in his eyes and Neatie went to the fridge and got some milk and washed his eyes with it. Chief was fine afterwards and carried on as usual.

Annita Cole

I'm Peggy Peugot and as I said , I'm parked by the house. I had nothing to do after that so I thought about Psalm 4:8 which says "In peace I will lie down and sleep, for you alone,O Lord, will keep me safe.

Spark Plugs

This is Peggy again and yes we are on the road again. Today we are near Namitete on a narrow road with dips. Where the road gets washed out the government puts dips with concrete in them. The water can still flow across but doesn't wash the road out.

We are coming to a big dip now. I got to the middle of it and I quit working. Neatie got out, opened my bonnet (hood) and wiped my spark plugs off with a dry cloth. Then she got back in the car,wet feet and all. I started back up and off we went. When my spark plugs get wet I stop. My spark plugs emit a bolt of electricity across a small gap igniting the fuel and air mixture that puts the pistons in motion and gets my motor running. This reminds me of the Holy Spirit and humans. When the humans take a leap of faith into the unknown and believe that Jesus died for them, then the Holy Spirit is ignited in their lives and they receive power to live God's way and boldness to tell others what Jesus has done for everyone. (Acts 1:8)

When my spark plugs get wet the moisture prevents the spark from flying across the gap to ignite the fuel and air mixture. I think sometimes humans let doubts and troubles keep them from the faith they need to jump the gap. Also at other times after they have made the leap of faith , they get discouraged and stop running for Jesus. That's when other humans need to encourage them and dry off their spark plugs. This will ignite their faith and keep them living for Jesus.

   To you kids reading this , I want you to read God's word and listen to the Holy Spirit and then you can keep on living for Jesus like I got going again after Neatie dried off my Spark Plugs.
I hope I will be able to talk to you again but goodbye for now.

a Big Surprise in the Dark

Hi I'm Peggy, coming to talk to you again. Right now I'm racing down the road in the dark and all seems well. I'm watching for things on the road in the headlights as we come over a hill I could see a lot of eyes staring at me in the dark. Neatie put my brakes on and blew my horn as we approached. I thought I was going to get messed up and kill a lot of sheep.To my surprise the sheep parted in the middle as we swept along. The sheep didn't get hurt and neither did we. I didn't get any damage on my body at all. I heard Neatie say to Izzy that she wouldn't have believed that if she hadn't seen it with her own eyes.

It was a warm place on a cold night and the sheep bedded down there not knowing how dangerous it was. God sure looked after us that time.In 2 Samuel 22:8 it says God is our shield, and the power that saves me.

Annita Cole

a Scary Moment

Hi kids and yes I'm back again. It is none other than Peggy. I have another story to tell you and this one is scary.

Neatie walked by me heading for the garage when a small, skinny, black dog came around the corner snarling with foam dripping from its mouth. Neatie knew what that meant . She knew that little dog had rabies.She looked really scared and just stood and stared at it. Then she hollered for help and grabbed a stick. One of the men went with her and together they killed it. They got rid of the dog and then washed up. If you get any of the saliva in a sore or broken skin then you can get it yourself. At the time this happened you could get vaccinations if you had been bit but they didn't guarantee them.

The minister of the church on the station had a son called Yotum. One night his little dog wanted in so he opened the door and got bit by a rabid dog which is why his dog wanted in. His father took him to the hospital a mile away for ten days to get the shot. One shot a day in the stomach. He survived and we were all happy. This little boy is now the pastor of the church on Mpanda station, 2 Samuel 22: 5 tells us that God is our refuge, our Savior, the one who saves us from violence.

Monkeys

Once again it was Sunday and we were on our way down to a church by the lake. My name is Peggy and I am a car. It's the dry hot season and so we can get to where we are going without getting stuck.

It is taking us a long time to get to Namilaza and we are enjoying the scenery. We just went by a large tree and new woven baskets were hanging in the branches. The people wanted us to buy one but we didn't need any so we didn't stop.

When we reached the church there wasn't anyone there. We waited and waited and waited some more. Finally around noon the people came. They told us they had been up all night keeping the monkeys from destroying their crops of corn. When the monkeys left they went home and got ready for church.

It is really hard to protect their crops where the monkeys are. The monkeys go down the rows of corn and keep picking. They put one under an arm and pick another. As they put the new cob under that arm the first one falls on the ground. They keep doing this until their crop is ruined.

They set up platforms to sleep on and one stays on guard. When the monkeys come they chase them away. This keeps on until they can harvest the crop. A hard way to farm but that is where they live and so that's what they do.

It sounded like they had a good church service and those people could really sing. It is so good to see these people in these mud and brick churches praising God and learning what God is saying to them. They are very happy people even in the midst of all their troubles.

Annita Cole

Phil 4:4 and 6 tell us to always be full of joy in the Lord and not to worry about anything but to pray about everything. I guess that's why these people by the lake can rejoice in spite of the monkeys.

Thank you for completing this book.

We would love if you could help by posting a review at your book retailer and on the PageMaster Publishing site. It only takes a minute and it would really help others by giving them an idea of your experience.

Thanks

Annita Cole at the PageMaster Store
https://pagemasterpublishing.ca/by/annita-cole/

To order more copies of this book, find books by other Canadian authors, or make inquiries about publishing your own book, contact PageMaster at:

PageMaster Publication Services Inc.
11340-120 Street, Edmonton, AB T5G 0W5
books@pagemaster.ca
780-425-9303

catalogue and e-commerce store
PageMasterPublishing.ca/Shop